21st Century
Basic Skills
Library

WE HARVEST APPLES IN FALL

by Rebecca Felix

Cherry Lake Publishing • Ann Arbor, Michigan

1

CHERRY
LAKE
Publishing

Published in the United States of America
by Cherry Lake Publishing
Ann Arbor, Michigan
www.cherrylakepublishing.com

Consultant: Marla Conn, Read-Ability

Photo Credits: Peter Mukherjee/iStockphoto, cover, 1; Doug Lemke/
Shutterstock Images, 4; Dennis Donohue/Shutterstock Images, 6;
Shutterstock Images, 8; Fedorov Oleksiy/Shutterstock Images, 10;
iStockphoto, 12; Joe Michl/iStockphoto, 14; Olga Lyubkina/Shutterstock
Images, 16; CandyBox Images/Shutterstock Images, 18; Mark Sauerwein/
iStockphoto, 20

Library of Congress Cataloging-in-Publication Data
Felix, Rebecca, 1984-
  We harvest apples in fall / Rebecca Felix.
      p. cm. -- (Let's look at fall)
  Includes index.
  ISBN 978-1-61080-905-4 (hardback : alk. paper) -- ISBN 978-1-61080-
930-6 (paperback : alk. paper) -- ISBN 978-1-61080-955-9 (ebook) -- ISBN
978-1-61080-980-1 (hosted ebook)
  1. Apples--Juvenile literature. 2. Apples--Harvesting--Juvenile literature.
3. Autumn--Juvenile literature. I. Title. II. Series: Felix, Rebecca, 1984- Let's
look at fall.

  SB363.F39 2013
  634'.11--dc23

                                     2012030458

Cherry Lake Publishing would like to acknowledge
the work of The Partnership for 21st Century Skills.
Please visit *www.21stcenturyskills.org* for more information.

Printed in the United States of America
Corporate Graphics Inc.
January 2013
CLFA10

TABLE OF CONTENTS

4

Fall Arrives

Fall is here. Weather cools.
Leaves turn colors.

Apple trees change in fall. The apples they grow change.

What Do You See?

Apples are in the same plant family as roses!

Apples Grow

Apples start as **blossoms**.
They **bloom** in summer. They
become fruit.

What Do You See?

How many apples do you see?

By fall, apples are **ripe**. They are ready to **harvest**.

Apple Season

To harvest apples is to pick
them. Workers pick many
apples.

Paul visits apple **orchards** in fall. He picks apples, too!

Apples are used to make many foods. Apple cider is made from pressed apples.

What Do You See?

What do you need to make apple pie?

18

Ann buys apples to take home. She makes apple pie.

Snowfall

Apple harvest is a special time. What season comes next?

Find Out More

BOOK

McNamara, Margaret. *Picking Apples*. New York: Aladdin-Simon & Schuster, 2009.

WEB SITE

Crispy's Apple Stand—Washington Apple Commission
www.bestapples.com/kids
Find fun apple facts, activities, and recipes.

Glossary

bloom (BLOOM) to become a flower

blossoms (BLAH-suhms) flowers on a seed plant, such as a fruit tree

harvest (HAHR-vist) to gather crops

orchards (OR-chards) collections of trees that grow fruit.

ripe (RIPE) full-grown and ready to be eaten

Home and School Connection

Use this list of words from the book to help your child become a better reader. Word games and writing activities can help beginning readers reinforce literacy skills.

apple	cools	orchards	time
arrives	fall	pick	trees
bloom	fruit	pie	visits
blossoms	grow	ripe	weather
buys	harvest	season	workers
change	home	snowfall	
cider	leaves	special	
color	make	summer	

What Do You See?

What Do You See? is a feature paired with select photos in this book. It encourages young readers to interact with visual images in order to build the ability to integrate content in various media formats.

You can help your child further evaluate photos in this book with additional activities. Look at the images in the book without the What Do You See? feature. Ask your child to describe one detail in each image, such as a color, food, activity, or setting.

Index

About the Author

Rebecca Felix is an editor and writer from Minnesota. She visits apple orchards there in fall. Her favorite fall drink is hot apple cider. She adds cinnamon for spice!